What if?

Questions to inspire, provoke thought and
expand your consciousness

———

Nereeda McInnes

Copyright © 2021 by Nereeda McInnes

All rights reserved.

No part of this book may be reproduced in any form or by any electronic or mechanical means, including information storage and retrieval systems, without written permission from the author, except for the use of brief quotations in a book review.

Cover design by David Provolo

First Printing, 2021

Ebook 978-0-6480541-9-1

Paperback 978-0-6480541-8-4

CONTENTS

Introduction	vii
How to use this book	ix
What if?	1
About the Author	287
Connect	289
More	291

Stay curious.

Introduction

I certainly don't have all the answers. Nor would I claim to. I do love a good question though.

Asking questions is how we grow.

It's how we expand.

It's how we connect with ourselves, and others, on a deeper level.

I believe we must ask questions often and seek our own truths.

We must learn to unlearn and remain open to new ideas, knowledge and information.

We must never stop learning.

We must never stop connecting with our heart.

And we must always keep going.

This is how we evolve.

This is how we awaken.

How to use this book

Read from cover to cover or flick to a random page for some "What if" inspiration. You may like to jot down your notes and insights on each page, in a notebook, or simply sit and ponder a question at a time. Whatever rings your bells, floats your boat or tickles your fancy. You got this.

NEREEDA MCINNES

What if you kept it simple?

What if the purpose of it all is to remember who you are?

What if the ultimate goal is to simply be and embody love?

WHAT IF?

What if your role is to do the work on yourself, develop your self-awareness and be your own leader?

NEREEDA MCINNES

What if you did the things you love?

WHAT IF?

What if you supported yourself as much as you support those dearest to you?

NEREEDA MCINNES

What if you let your light shine and stopped giving a flying f*ck about what other people think? In a loving way, of course.

WHAT IF?

What if you never forgot to laugh?

What if that noise coming from the elderly lady in the grocery store wasn't the wheels of her trolley?

WHAT IF?

What if we were more honest with ourselves?

What if we sang like no one was watching?
You know, loud, proud at the top of our lungs sang.

What if the conspiracy was true all along?

What if we explored more of who we are?

What if farts are funny in every dimension?

What if you had all that you needed within you right now to do the thing you know in your heart you are here to do?

WHAT IF?

What if, when you work on yourself, you are healing not only yourself but past, present and future generations too?

What if we changed understand to innerstand? So, rather than standing under something, we feel it deep inside.

WHAT IF?

What if when we live in the NOW, we reverse it and realise we have WON?

What if we all rocked the ripple (aka: created a positive ripple effect) in our own unique way? #rocktheripple

What if the goal is to awaken?

What if the only way through is within?

WHAT IF?

What if we just let go, danced like no one was watching and went a bit silly for a while?

What if we remembered that we are all made up of energy and moving particles?

What if you can heal others by healing yourself?

What if our positive frequencies had been hijacked and reversed to control the powerful creatures that we are?

What if we took the word EVIL and reversed it? How would you LIVE?

What if when you live your truth and stand in your power, that is when the true miracles happen?

What if all answers lie within?

What if you just sat with it for a while?

WHAT IF?

What if you loved the parts of yourself that you don't like?

What if our reality had been inverted and our job was to flip it back into balance?

What if we listened to understand not to respond?

What if we included more puns on a daily basis? That would be pretty punny wouldn't it? Or would it...?

WHAT IF?

What if we loved ourselves so deeply that we could never intentionally hurt another?

NEREEDA MCINNES

What if this is all one big experiment?

WHAT IF?

What if we truly saw the beauty in a single moment?

What if we remembered to pause and take a deep breath?

WHAT IF?

What if we allowed ourselves to feel our feelings—the good, the bad, the ugly?

What if you said "no"?

What if you said "yes"?

What if you honoured the process?

WHAT IF?

What if, when we were having a busy or crappy day, we all stopped and had a dance break? You know, maybe just for a minute or two while at home or waiting in the line at the supermarket or post office.

What if we implemented said dance break
from here on in? #dancebreak #doingitnow

What if we paid more attention to the signs?

What if, what makes you uncomfortable in others, is a reflection of what needs to be healed or explored within yourself?

What if you decided to love yourself?

What if you forgave yourself?

What if you forgave others?

What if, the more you know, the more you realise you don't know?

What if everything comes down to relationships—with yourself, others, nature, food, source, etc?

What if we remembered that we are multidimensional beings with the power to create our own reality? What would you create?

What if we questioned the narrative?

What if we questioned our own beliefs, ideas and thought patterns?

What if we are here to raise our vibration and shift consciousness?

NEREEDA MCINNES

What if this is what you came here for?

What if we stopped comparing our life story to that of others? Are we not all writing a different story anyway?

What if focusing on only love and light
isn't the answer?

What if focusing on only the positive is just as detrimental as focusing on only the negative?

What if we looked at both sides of the coin?

What if, when your partner, friend or family member came home from work for the day, you did a welcome home dance for them?

What if true power comes from within?

What if, in order to transform the world, we must transform ourselves?

What if everything begins within?

WHAT IF?

What if we dealt with our childhood trauma?

What if we let go of what is no longer serving us so we can be all we came here to be?

What if we remembered that one small act of kindness can create a positive ripple effect on a scale larger than we could ever imagine?

What if we got to know ourselves on a deeper level? And when we did that, we went deeper again?

What if the goal is to de-program the program?

What if we are here to thrive, not just survive?

What if we remembered the power of who we really are?

What if we did the thing for no other reason than to do it? Not for fame, not for kudos, not for recognition—but to just to do it.

What if we noticed the … s p a c e … between our thoughts?

What if we remembered that we are sovereign beings?

WHAT IF?

What if the most fantastic movies ever made were based on truth, not fiction?

What if you took a deep breath, dropped into your heart and felt for a moment the truth of who you really are?

WHAT IF?

What if each challenge you were faced with was an opportunity to grow?

What if we loved and respected ourselves so much, we could never not do the same for another?

WHAT IF?

What if we saw the humour of it all? Or humor if you are in the US.

NEREEDA MCINNES

What if we weren't so serious all the time?

What if we remembered to dance?

What if we stopped watching the news, the program-ing, the 'tell-a-vision'?

WHAT IF?

What if you are here to shine your light in the only way you can?

What if you helped someone else today?

What if it's true?

What if, when something doesn't feel quite right or you feel a shift within, you ask yourself, is this mine?

What if the true heroes of this world will never be known on a grand scale?

… NEREEDA MCINNES

What if we asked better questions?

WHAT IF?

What if we noticed our initial thoughts before reacting? And, what if we sat with them for a while before deciding what action to take, if any?

What if the greatest story ever told is playing out in real time, right now, and only those with eyes to see it are enjoying the show?

What if you had a choice about what side of history you want to be on? What if you already do?

What if it isn't true?

What if you're wrong?

What if you are exactly where you need to be?

WHAT IF?

What if we asked ourselves "what if" more often?

What if we asked more questions?

What if that emotion you are feeling is the 'energy-in-motion' that is ready to be acknowledged and released?

What if every time you walked past a mirror or saw yourself in a reflection, you gave yourself a wink and a nod?

WHAT IF?

What if you got out of your own way?

What if you stood in your power?

WHAT IF?

What if it doesn't have to be that hard?

What if it could be simple?

What if we laughed more? You know, the laugh so hard a little bit of pee might come out kind of laugh?

What if we forgot who we are and our role is to remember?

What if magic is real and we were tricked into thinking it wasn't, so that only a small group of people who know and believe in magic could control the world?

What if we created the game in order to play it?

WHAT IF?

What if instead of saying "why me", we said "what is this trying to teach me"?

What if wisdom is healed trauma?

WHAT IF?

What if the only way out is in?

What if, when something bothers us, we asked ourselves why it bothered us so much in the first place?

WHAT IF?

What if you could say one thing to the entire world? What would you say?

What if you said "enough is enough—I AM DOING THIS"?

WHAT IF?

What if you just said 'f*ck it'?

What if you shining your light serves humanity in more ways than you could ever know?

WHAT IF?

What if you said yes to living in alignment with your highest good?

What if we imagined a new reality—one with no suffering and freedom for all?

WHAT IF?

What if, together, we willed in the best outcome for all of humanity?

What if we awakened to our true potential?

What if we decided to change the game?

NEREEDA MCINNES

What if we had more fun?

WHAT IF?

What if, every time you smile at a stranger, you also winked and said "pull my finger"?

What if we brought the joy wherever possible?

What if we relished in being exactly who we are?

NEREEDA MCINNES

What if we played more?

What if the game has only just begun?

What if when we close our eyes this is when we truly see?

WHAT IF?

What if it didn't matter if we didn't understand the question? What if we just sat with it and allowed it to be whatever it needed to be for us in that moment?

What if we got braver? Even just a bit…

WHAT IF?

What if, when you asked your partner if they wanted a cup of tea, you did a "do you want a cup of tea dance"?

What if you took just one small step at a time?

What if 'making the best of things' is the best thing?

What if you are afraid to teach what you know because you are worried about getting something wrong even though we all know none of us will ever get it right 100% of the time? What if someone misses out on what they needed to hear from you because of it?

What if you literally did stop to smell the roses?

What if you listened to other people's point of view—not to agree or disagree, but to get a feel for where they are coming from and why they hold that perspective in the first place?

WHAT IF?

What if the truth will set you free, but first it will freak you the hell out, then put a fire in your belly so strong that you can't help but want to usher in an amazing new world for humanity?

What if there is only one truth?

WHAT IF?

What if, every time we thought we already knew something, we asked ourselves, "what more can I learn here"?

What if the real reason that Tommy couldn't ride the bike was because he was a fish?

WHAT IF?

What if we had access to repressed technology? What would you create, heal, imagine?

What if, when we are feeling stuck or helpless in our own life, we set out to help another?

What if you waited?

What if you took action right now? What one step would you take?

What if we were willing to look at the tough stuff?

What if we stood up for what we truly believe in?

What if we could see the possibility?

NEREEDA MCINNES

What if we were willing to explore?

WHAT IF?

What if we came here to unlearn?

What if everything you were taught to believe was a lie?

What if what mattered most was truth, love, joy and freedom?

NEREEDA MCINNES

What if there is more truth in movies than you ever thought possible?

What if we followed universal law (lore) in the simplest of ways i.e. 'do not harm another'?

What if every time you saw someone walk into a room you asked them "what are yoooouuu doing" in a curious voice?

What if you had all the money you ever needed? What would you do?

What if you respected yourself 100%? Would you ever disrespect another?

What if we realised the infinite possibility of 'all that is'?

What if you are the 'all that is'?

WHAT IF?

What if we decided to love ourselves?

What if we've been asking the wrong questions?

WHAT IF?

What if we went where we were celebrated, not just tolerated?

What if due to the fact that our human eye can only see a very small percentage of the light spectrum, there are multitudes of dimensions and realities existing in the very same plane humans do, only we aren't able to see it with our own eyes?

What if when someone was having one of "those" days you went up to them and said, "pull my finger", and when they did you said, "you rock!" Side-note: This action may depend on the kind of one of "those" days they are having and who you are talking to. Perhaps a "beep-beep' would be more appropriate. I'll leave with to you to decide…

What if you knew better?

WHAT IF?

What if you said, "I'm sorry"?

What if you forgave yourself for the things you wish you could change?

WHAT IF?

What if you remembered that everyone makes mistakes and there's not one person on this planet, with a heart, that wouldn't change something or do something differently given the opportunity?

What if you could see how important you being exactly who you are is in the grand scheme of things?

What if there are no mistakes?

What if we create our own fate?

WHAT IF?

What if we create our reality?

What if our thoughts, feelings, emotions and actions are more important than we ever realised?

What if you went with that decision? How does it feel?

What if you didn't run with that decision?
How does that feel?

What if we never forgot that we are all connected—each of us, one part of the whole?

What if there was something new to be learned here?

What if you pondered the question, "why not me"?

What if you were to surrender that which you cannot control?

WHAT IF?

What if you allowed your life to flow with ease and grace wherever possible?

NEREEDA MCINNES

What if you remained open to all possibilities?

WHAT IF?

What if there is another way?

What if your triggers are showing you what needs to be healed?

What if what you judge in others is something you judge about yourself that you may or may not be aware of?

What if you could be the observer?

What if we thought for ourselves—even more?

NEREEDA MCINNES

What if we became better critical thinkers?

WHAT IF?

What if we didn't have all the answers?

What if when we needed to let off steam or 'crack the sh*ts', there was a dedicated 'crack the sh*ts' area in our home, workplace or office? (I first heard this idea years ago. A radio presenter thought this would be a good idea for tennis players who seem to always be getting upset and yelling at the umpire all the time.)

WHAT IF?

What if we could trust the process?

NEREEDA MCINNES

What if we could trust ourselves?

What if we are here to experience it all?

What if we have been everything that has ever been or ever will be?

WHAT IF?

What if the truth is hidden in plain sight?

What if you let go of that thing you have been holding onto—you know, the thing that has been holding you back from being all that you are?

What if you chose better?

What if you could love yourself just as you are?

WHAT IF?

What if you could forgive yourself for those things you haven't forgiven yourself for just yet?

What if we turned everything into a song? Even just for a day. We could totally incorporate this with the #dancebreak as seen on page 42-43.

WHAT IF?

What if, even if you don't know what you need to do to make a change in your life, you were willing to take the first step?

What if you could go with the flow?

WHAT IF?

What if you weren't always wishing you were somewhere else and could just be where you are?

What if having your back against the wall was allowing you to do the things you didn't think you could?

WHAT IF?

What if it didn't have to be that way?

What if, when we did a sneaky fart in the car and lifted our butt off the seat, we had to stay lifted or the person in the car next to us would realise we had just farted?

What if we asked ourselves—"will this really matter in 5 years"?

What if you could let it go?

What if the universe is you?

What if what we do to others is what we do to ourselves?

What if nothing matters?

NEREEDA MCINNES

What if everything is just as it should be?

WHAT IF?

What if we are shifting timelines?

What if you really are a magnificent creature who is powerful beyond measure?

What if you changed your mind?

NEREEDA MCINNES

What if this moment really is all that matters?

What if your challenges were your greatest gifts?

What if you were meant to experience that?

What if you could start over? What would you do?

What if you let your intuition guide you?

WHAT IF?

What if you followed your heart?

What if your decisions affected your past, present and future?

What if time is an illusion?

What if we are living in one giant 'Truman Show'?

What if magic is real—whether you believe in it or not?

What if truth really is stranger than fiction?

WHAT IF?

What if you created this? All of it?

What if everything is coming together for your highest good and in ways you could never possibly imagine?

What if you became your own hero?

NEREEDA MCINNES

What if we had it backwards?

What if there is something more?

NEREEDA MCINNES

What if we did our own research?

What if we were more discerning?

What if, once you are aware, there is no turning back?

WHAT IF?

What if every time we left work for the day we said "I'm off like a fart in the wind"? Sidenote: A friend used to say that very thing at the end of the day in the office and she really did breeze right out of there!

What if you are the answer?

What if there is a cure?

What if we didn't take it for granted—the people in our lives, the information we have been told, the stories that have been shared?

What if, we changed "should" to "I will" or "I won't?"

What if perception isn't reality?

What if you looked at why you were so offended in the first place?

What if you were more honest with yourself?

What if it could only be seen when we let go of what we thought we knew?

What if they're not as crazy as you think?

What if it was meant to be this way?

What if the power of choice is the biggest gift we have?

What if we are here to raise the vibration of the planet?

What if we chose love over fear?

What if we are on the verge of creating heaven on earth and the power to do so is in our hands?

What if you did the stuff you are passionate about?

What if money was no longer needed?

What if, when you got to 80 years old and looked back on your life you had a choice of saying, "what if?" or "what a ride?" What do you want to be saying?

WHAT IF?

What if your body is powerful enough to heal itself?

What if you looked at it from another point of view?

What if that thing you find so easy is actually one of your biggest gifts?

What if that pain you are feeling is showing you what is ready to be healed?

WHAT IF?

What if that thing you can't stop thinking about is in your heart because it is what you are here to do?

What if you chose your name before you were born?

WHAT IF?

What if every moment was an opportunity to create a new reality?

What if you said "no" when it wasn't a "hell yes"?

What if there are more layers than we could ever imagine?

NEREEDA MCINNES

What if every sneeze led to a fart?

WHAT IF?

What if you did more of what you crave?

What if, when we wanted more, we gave to others?

What if we created this?

What if you asked yourself what you are most afraid of, and why?

What if the most important relationship you will ever have is the one you have with yourself?

What if life is a movie—one big hero's journey?

What if we spoke in different accents sometimes just for fun? #youknowIdo (spoken in an British accent)

NEREEDA MCINNES

What if, for all the dark, there is the most beautiful light you could ever imagine?

WHAT IF?

What if there is more beyond this matrix?

NEREEDA MCINNES

What if you didn't wait for permission and just 'did the damn thing'?

What if you are more than you think you are?

What if we fall so we can learn to get back up?

What if we are here to move from "I am" to "we are"?

What if we could all bring a lil' bit more #norman into our lives? As seen here: nereedamcinnes.com/norman

What if standing up for ourselves looks different for everyone?

NEREEDA MCINNES

What if we re-imagined our reality?

WHAT IF?

What if you are the miracle?

What if your energy is just too much for some
—but bloody incredible for others?

WHAT IF?

What if we are all being watched in this big movie of life?

What if, when a cyclist rides past you on your morning walk and yells out "passing", you reply with "wind"?

What if we remembered what we wanted to be when we grew up?

What if you didn't have to prove yourself to anyone?

WHAT IF?

What if we focused on the solution, not the problem?

NEREEDA MCINNES

What if we were more patient?

WHAT IF?

What if we respected our breath more?

NEREEDA MCINNES

What if we said "we before me?"

What if we encouraged each other more?

What if we sung our conversations?

WHAT IF?

What if you had the power all along?

About the Author

Nereeda McInnes is a bestselling author, mentor, podcast host and founder and creator of numerous frequency-shifting tools, products and programs. As an explorer of many different healing modalities, she is also a passionate advocate for personal development, transformation and knowing ourselves at a deeper level. Bringing a unique mix of spirituality, humour and realism to all that she does, Nereeda is on a mission to see humanity thrive and loves working with people who feel that too.

Connect at these places ↓

Website

nereedamcinnes.com

Social

@nereedamcinnes

Also by Nereeda McInnes

The Truth of Your Reality
Insights on the game of life and how you choose to play it.

Available at:
nereedamcinnes.com/books

www.ingramcontent.com/pod-product-compliance
Lightning Source LLC
Chambersburg PA
CBHW070248010526
44107CB00056B/2390